THE STORY OF MISTY COPELAND

A Biography Book for New Readers

Written by
Frank Berrios

Illustrated by
Juanita Londoño

ROCKRIDGE PRESS

To the four amazing women who inspired me to become a reader and a writer: Darma, Yolanda, Norma, and Stephanie.

For general information on our other products and services or to obtain technical support, please contact our Customer Care Department within the United States at (866) 744-2665, or outside the United States at (510) 253-0500.

Rockridge Press publishes its books in a variety of electronic and print formats. Some content that appears in print may not be available in electronic books, and vice versa.

Series Designer: Angela Navarra
Interior and Cover Designer: Elizabeth Zuhl
Art Producer: Hannah Dickerson
Editor: Erum Khan
Production Editor: Ruth Sakata Corley
Production Manager: Riley Hoffman

Illustrations © 2021 Juanita Londoño; all maps used under license from Creative Market. Photography © The Photo Access/Alamy Stock Photo, p. 50; Lev Radin/Shutterstock.com, p. 52; ZUMA Press, Inc./Alamy Stock Photo, p. 53. Author photo courtesy of Mike Meskin. Illustrator photo courtesy of Santiago Alzate.

Paperback ISBN: 978-1-63807-499-1 | eBook ISBN: 978-1-63878-014-4
R0
Printed in China

CONTENTS

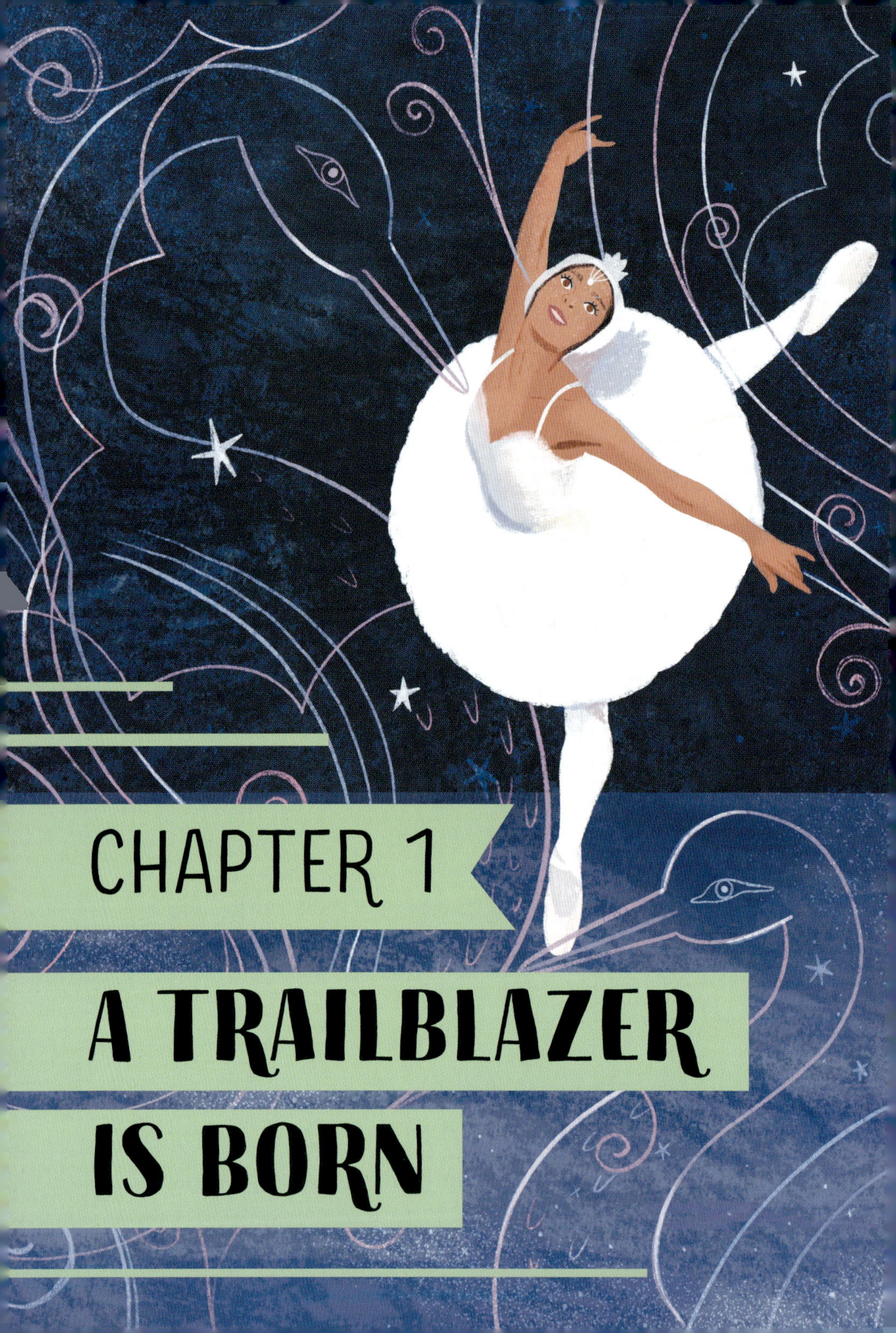

CHAPTER 1

A TRAILBLAZER IS BORN

Meet Misty Copeland

As a shy girl growing up in California, Misty Copeland never thought that she would go on to become a talented, strong, and graceful ballet dancer. She didn't know she would touch people's hearts with her movements on the stage. She couldn't have predicted that she would travel around the globe and inspire millions of little girls and boys to follow in her footsteps. But as the first female African American **principal dancer** at American Ballet Theatre, that's exactly what she did!

Misty went from eating dinner out of vending machines to being **appointed** to the President's Council on Fitness, Sports & Nutrition by President Barack Obama! With her positive outlook on life, Misty became a role model and inspiration to dancers around the world. She changed the lives of countless people, simply by

proving that she belonged alongside the world's best **ballerinas**, even though she looked nothing like most of them.

After being encouraged to join a **ballet** class as a young teenager, Misty quickly rose to the top of the **classical** ballet world. But it wasn't easy. Though she was a naturally gifted dancer, Misty still had to work hard to achieve her dreams. And she hasn't stopped yet! Misty has written books and been featured in magazines, including *Time* and *Vogue*. She's appeared in music videos, movies, and on Broadway. There's even a Misty Copeland Barbie® doll! Misty's amazing achievements and incredible life story continue to inspire people every day. She encourages children of all races, body shapes, and sizes to follow their dreams—and to dance!

Misty's World

Misty Danielle Copeland was born in Kansas City, Missouri, on September 10, 1982. She was her mother Sylvia's fourth child. Misty had an older sister named Erica, and two older

brothers named Doug Jr. and Chris. Not long after Misty was born, she welcomed two more **siblings** to the family—a sister named Lindsey and younger brother, Cameron, the baby of the bunch.

Misty is part of a multiracial family, which means they have **ancestors** that come from many **cultures** and places around the world. Misty's father was the son of a German woman and an African American man. And Misty's mom was the daughter of an African American man and an Italian woman.

> "I've never strayed away from being Black. I'm biracial but something that my mom constantly said to me growing up in southern California was 'Yes, you are Italian, you are German, and you are Black, but you are going to be viewed by the world as a Black woman.'"

When Misty was born, there weren't many African Americans involved in the world of classical ballet. Ballet dancers usually start training when they are very young. Ballet classes can also be expensive. Ballet equipment like shoes, **leotards**, and **tights** can cost a lot of money. Ballet audiences weren't very diverse, either. Tickets could often be pricey, so it

was considered entertainment mostly for rich white people. Because of this, most professional ballet dancers were white. That might be why Misty was never introduced to ballet as a young girl.

With six mouths to feed, Misty's mom didn't always have money left over at the end of each week for extra stuff like ballet classes. Misty may not have known much about the ballet world, but soon enough she would become one of its biggest and brightest stars!

JUMP IN THE THINK TANK

If you could live somewhere else, where would you go? What do you think you would enjoy the most about living in a different city or town?

WHEN?

SEPTEMBER 10, 1982 — Misty Copeland is born in Kansas City, Missouri.

AROUND 1984 — Misty's mom moves the family to California.

CHAPTER 2

THE EARLY YEARS

Moving Around

When Misty was just two years old, her parents got a **divorce**. Misty's mom decided to move her kids to California. It took two long days to make the bus trip, but Misty and her siblings soon settled into a small apartment. Misty's mom remarried a year after they arrived in California. Misty enjoyed living with her new stepdad, Harold. He loved to spend time with Misty, watching TV and sharing sunflower seeds, one of her favorite snacks.

When Misty's mother broke up with Harold, the family moved again. This time, instead of a small apartment, they lived in a big house that overlooked the ocean! Unfortunately, Misty's family didn't stay there long, either. The family eventually moved into a little motel in San Pedro. The room was so small that Misty and her siblings had to sleep on the couch and floor. Misty was embarrassed about living in a motel, so she didn't tell her friends where she lived.

Life wasn't all bad, though. When Misty was in grade school, she performed in a talent show with her sister Erica and her brother Chris. Misty seemed like she was born to be onstage. Misty's mother used to be a cheerleader for the Kansas City Chiefs football team, so most of her siblings were sports fans. Misty's favorite was always **gymnastics**.

MYTH & FACT

MYTH: All of the best ballerinas start dancing when they are less than 5 years old.

FACT: Misty took her very first ballet class when she was 13!

JUMP IN THE THINK TANK

What do you like to do after school? Do you play sports? Or do you like to stay inside, read books, or play video games?

After watching a movie about a famous gymnast named Nadia Comaneci, Misty began teaching herself how to do splits and cartwheels in the backyard. Those moves would come in handy when Misty tried out for the drill team in middle school. After weeks of practice, Misty performed her **solo**. She was by far the best dancer, so no one was surprised when she was named team captain!

The First Ballet Class

Misty loved being drill team captain. She liked to create and **choreograph** new dance moves. Misty always felt confident and strong when she was dancing. Her drill team coach, Elizabeth Cantine, noticed Misty's natural talent. She showed Misty some basic ballet moves.

While many dancers take years to learn things, Misty could quickly repeat steps just by watching.

Elizabeth had a friend who was teaching a ballet class at the San Pedro Boys & Girls Club. She asked Misty to take the class. Misty was nervous, so at first she just watched.

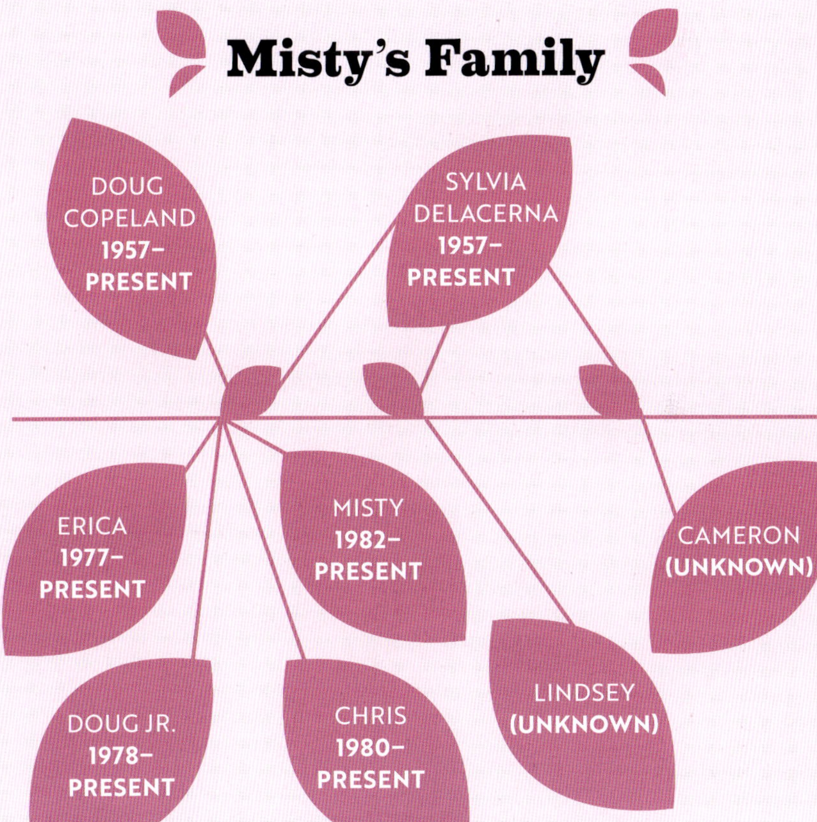

Finally, the teacher, Cindy Bradley, asked her to join in. Misty noticed she was much older than the other kids. Some had started taking ballet classes when they were just 3 years old. Misty was already 13! They were also wearing fancy tights, leotards, and ballet shoes. Misty wore a T-shirt and an old pair of shorts. She felt like she didn't fit in. Eventually, Misty got the courage to join the other kids in class.

For the next hour, Misty twisted her body, stretched her arms, and pointed her toes. She learned the five basic positions of ballet. At first, she thought it was boring. But Cindy saw that Misty had natural talent. She offered Misty a **scholarship** to her ballet school across town.

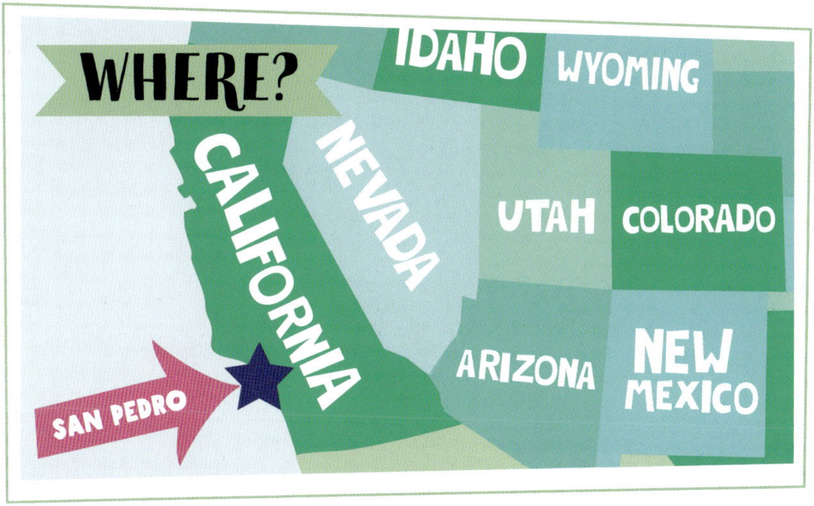

But when Misty started coming home very late, her mom had second thoughts. She thought ballet was taking up too much of Misty's time. She told her to quit. Misty was starting to love ballet, so she was heartbroken. Cindy came up with a **solution**. She offered to let Misty live with her, so she could get more rest and training.

Misty joins a drill team.

1995

Misty attends her first ballet class

1996

WHEN?

CHAPTER 3

BECOMING A BALLERINA

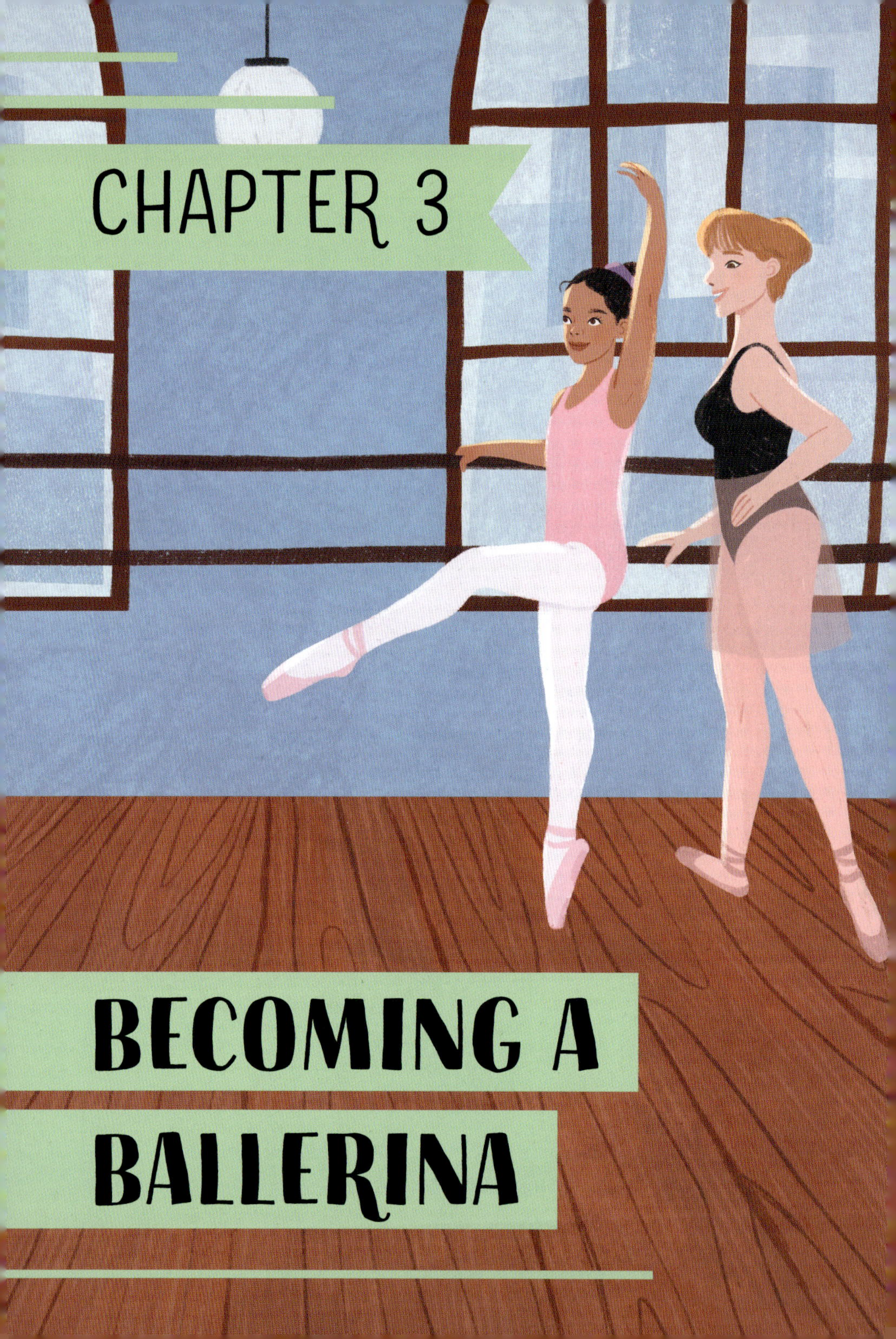

A New Life

Misty's new life with Cindy Bradley's family was completely different from the one she was used to. In Misty's family, there were six kids under one roof. There was always a noisy television on or a radio blaring music. Cindy's house, on the other hand, was quiet and calm. Misty was also used to eating potato chips and candy, but Cindy did not allow junk food in her home. Instead, Misty had to eat fresh fruits and vegetables.

The Bradleys also had lots of recordings of ballet **performances**. Misty watched dancers like Paloma Herrera perform with the American Ballet Theatre (ABT), a famous ballet company in New York City. Misty instantly fell in love with Paloma's flowing moves and leaps. She wanted to be just like her. Misty dreamed of one day dancing for the ABT.

Misty performed everywhere she could. She was asked to **audition** for the **lead** role in *Hot Chocolate Nutcracker*. This performance would feature Black dancers, as well as some traditional African dances. Although many people tried out, Misty got the part!

Misty's first big competition would be the Music Center's Spotlight Awards. With less than two years of training, she performed a difficult ballet routine—and won! The buzz from her win put her in a good position to audition for summer ballet programs. Each summer, the top ballet companies open their doors to teach young dancers and find new talent. Misty's dancing caught the attention of many companies. In the end, she decided to attend the summer program at the San Francisco Ballet, which was much closer to home than other programs in Chicago or New York. Misty enjoyed her time in San Francisco. She made new friends and went sightseeing. But soon, it was time to head back home.

JUMP —IN THE— THINK TANK

Is there something that you can do well, like dance or play sports? What can you do to get even better at those things?

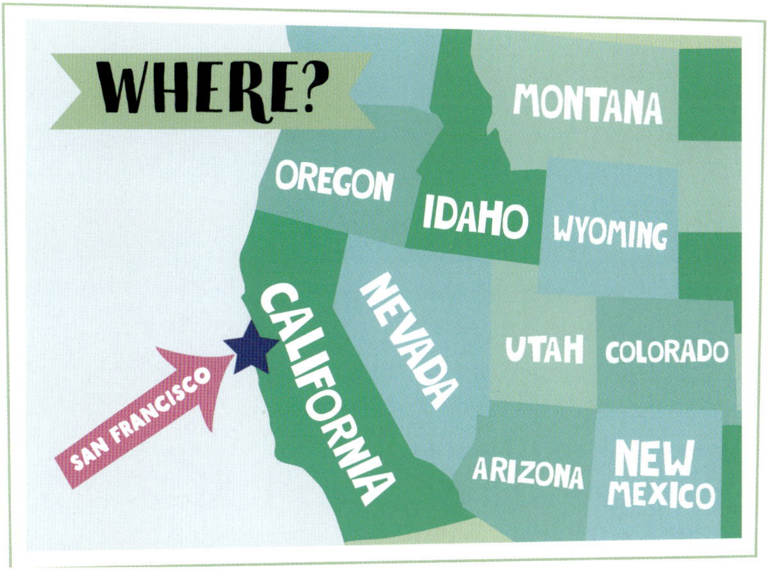

Ups and Downs

As Misty became busier and busier with ballet, she had less time to spend with her family. Misty was supposed to spend weekdays with the Bradleys and come home on weekends. But sometimes she was so busy she wouldn't come home from the Bradleys' house for weeks at a time. When she did, it was just for short visits. Misty's mother began to think that Cindy was trying to turn Misty against her. Before long, Sylvia wanted Misty to move back home. She also wanted Misty to find a new ballet school and teacher.

> "Dance exists in every culture, every age . . . I think it's the most natural thing that you can do."

Misty was sad. She loved the Bradleys, and she knew how much Cindy had taught her about ballet. Cindy was also upset. She introduced Misty to a lawyer who told Misty he could help her do whatever she wanted without her mother's permission. Misty would then be treated like an adult, even though she was still only 16 years old. At the courthouse, the lawyer asked a judge to let Misty make her own decisions about her life. The case dragged on for a while. She realized that both her mother and Cindy loved her very much. In the end, Misty decided to move back home and find a new ballet teacher.

At the new ballet studio, Misty quickly made friends. She also focused more on achieving her dreams of becoming a professional ballet dancer. Not long after, Misty's mom found a new job, allowing her to move the entire family into a new apartment. Once again, Misty began to feel hopeful about her future!

WHEN?

1996 — Misty moves in with her ballet coach, Cindy Bradley.

1997 — Misty wins first place in the Spotlight Awards.

1998 — Misty attends a ballet workshop in San Francisco.

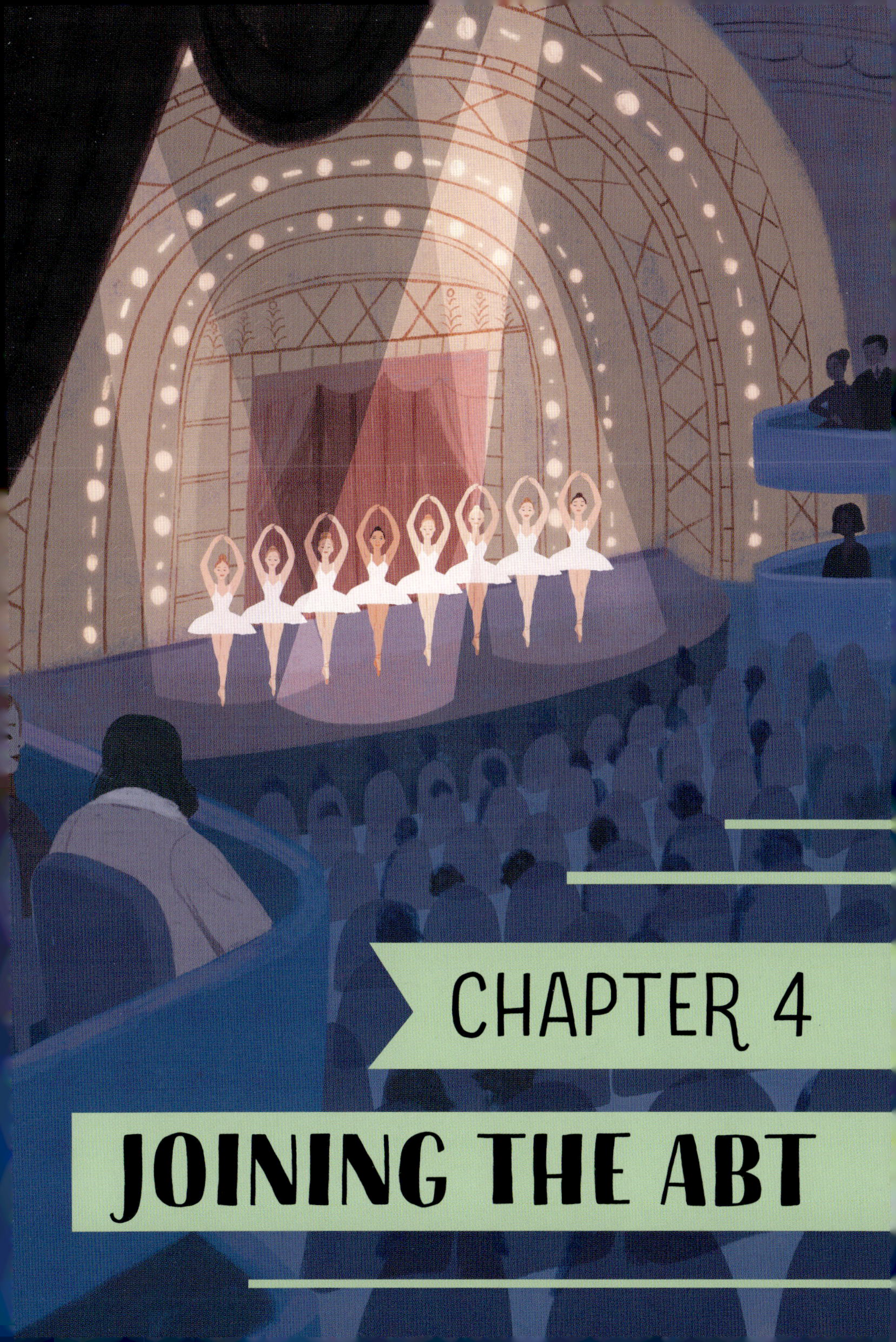

CHAPTER 4

JOINING THE ABT

The Only One

Misty had dreamed of joining the American Ballet Theatre (ABT) ever since she was 13 years old. ABT started in New York City in 1939. It is one of the greatest ballet companies in the world. Misty's idol, Paloma Herrera, was a dancer with ABT. Misty was overjoyed when she was accepted into the ABT summer program. She was also excited about living in New York! It felt like a fresh start.

Misty spent her days practicing, and the hard work paid off. At the end of the summer, John Meehan, the artistic director of the ABT Studio Company, invited her to join them. The Studio Company is a small group of dancers who train together to get ready to join the main group of ABT dancers. Misty was only 16, so she decided to go back to California to finish high school instead.

After graduating, Misty returned to New York, ready to dance. Two years later, Misty would be promoted to ABT's corps de ballet. The corps de ballet is an important part of a dance company that works as a team to support the dancers in the lead roles. Dancers in the corps de ballet aren't supposed to stand out. But as the only brown-skinned girl at ABT, Misty always stood out.

Misty often felt like she was alone in the world of ballet. Thankfully, she was inspired by

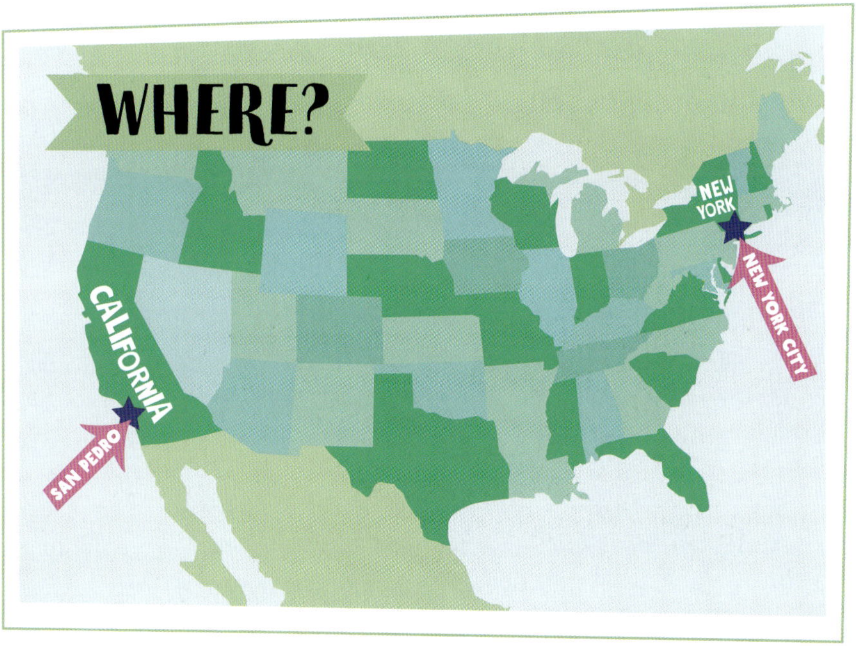

ballerinas who had come before her. Misty met Raven Wilkinson, a talented Black ballerina who was forced to leave the United States in the 1950s to find work. Before long, Raven became Misty's mentor.

★ Staying Strong ★

One night, while practicing for a show, Misty felt a sharp pain in her back. When she went to the doctor, she found out she had a stress fracture, which is a tiny crack in the bone. After an operation, Misty needed to wear a back brace 23 hours a day for six months! During that time, her body changed. Misty grew from a little girl

MYTH	&	FACT
Dancing is easy and doesn't take much work.		Dancers often rehearse, or practice, ten hours a day, six days a week!

with small shoulders to a young woman with hips and curves. Suddenly, the costumes Misty shared with other dancers were too tight. Misty was asked to lengthen, which was ABT's way of telling her to lose weight. Misty never had to worry about what she ate before, so she was embarrassed. It was a difficult time.

Misty decided to take a few classes outside ABT with Arthur Mitchell, cofounder of Dance Theatre of Harlem. As a Black dancer himself,

JUMP IN THE THINK TANK

Dancing is a great way to exercise and stay healthy. What are some other fun ways to stay active and fit?

Arthur understood Misty's concern about not looking like a "classical" ballerina. Instead of making her feel bad about her body, Arthur praised Misty's dancing and strength. He also offered her a role as a soloist. Although Misty was flattered, she didn't want to give up on her dream of becoming a principal dancer at ABT.

Misty had learned how to avoid unhealthy food and she always trained hard. ABT encouraged Misty's choices and soon realized that her curves were part of who she was and why she danced so well. They started focusing on her health instead of her body shape and weight.

Around this time, Misty met a handsome law student named Olu. The two dated, fell in love, and eventually married!

WHEN?

1999	2000	2001	2004
Misty attends ABT's summer workshop.	Misty graduates from high school and joins ABT.	Misty is promoted to the ABT corps de ballet.	Misty meets Olu, her future husband.

CHAPTER 5
A RISING STAR

New Opportunities

As Misty continued to grow as an artist, she began to think about her father. Misty hadn't seen her dad since she was two years old. She wasn't even sure what he looked like anymore. Thankfully, her brother Doug Jr. knew where their father lived. They went to visit him together.

Misty's dad wrapped his arms around her when they reunited. He shared stories over lunch about Misty's German grandmother and African American grandfather. Misty met other family members, like her grandfather's sister. Misty was inspired by the lives of her father's family. The trip made Misty realize how important family was to her.

When she returned to New York, Misty was even more determined to succeed at ABT. But problems would soon arise again. In ballets like *Swan Lake*, dancers often dust their faces with

JUMP IN THE THINK TANK

Misty wanted to learn more about her family. How can you do the same thing? Start by asking a family member to help you make a family tree!

white powder to make them look more ghostlike. Some people thought Misty shouldn't be allowed to dance in those roles. They thought her brown skin would be a distraction to the audience. Misty couldn't understand why the color of her skin was more important than her dancing.

Friends, family, and fans provided encouragement and kind words, which gave Misty the patience and strength to keep pushing. Misty knew that if she continued to work hard, her turn in the spotlight would come. That day arrived in 2007, when Misty was promoted to soloist! As the only African American dancer in the company, Misty was proud to be a symbol of change in the world of ballet. But she knew she still had much more work to do.

Flying Solo

Misty always loved music. When the famous musician Prince reached out to her about dancing in a music video, she couldn't say no. Misty choreographed her own dance moves for the video. Then Prince asked Misty to join him on tour in several countries, including France! Misty and Prince worked together to create a dance based on one of his most popular songs.

Misty had fun working with Prince, and she knew it was a great opportunity to share ballet with a whole new audience. Some Prince fans had probably never seen a true ballerina before.

Ballet had completely changed Misty's life, so she was eager to share that gift with others. Performing with Prince also gave her a boost of confidence. For the first time, she began to feel like an artist instead of just a student of ballet.

Misty was also able to meet her idol, Paloma Herrera! Misty had followed Paloma's accomplishments like others follow sports and movie stars. Misty mentioned how much she admired Paloma in a magazine article. Paloma was surprised and happy to learn that her dancing inspired Misty to become a ballerina. Years later, they would even become friends.

In 2012, Misty was inducted into the Boys & Girls Club Hall of Fame. Misty's mother, sisters, and brothers were all there, along with her former ballet teacher Cindy Bradley.

"As a dancer, performing is my life. When I can't dance, I feel lost."

Even her former drill team coach, Liz Cantine, was in the crowd! Misty was able to thank all of the people who had helped her achieve her dreams.

Misty is promoted to soloist in the ABT.

Misty is inducted into the Boys & Girls Club Hall of Fame.

WHEN? **2007** **2012**

CHAPTER 6

BREAKING BARRIERS

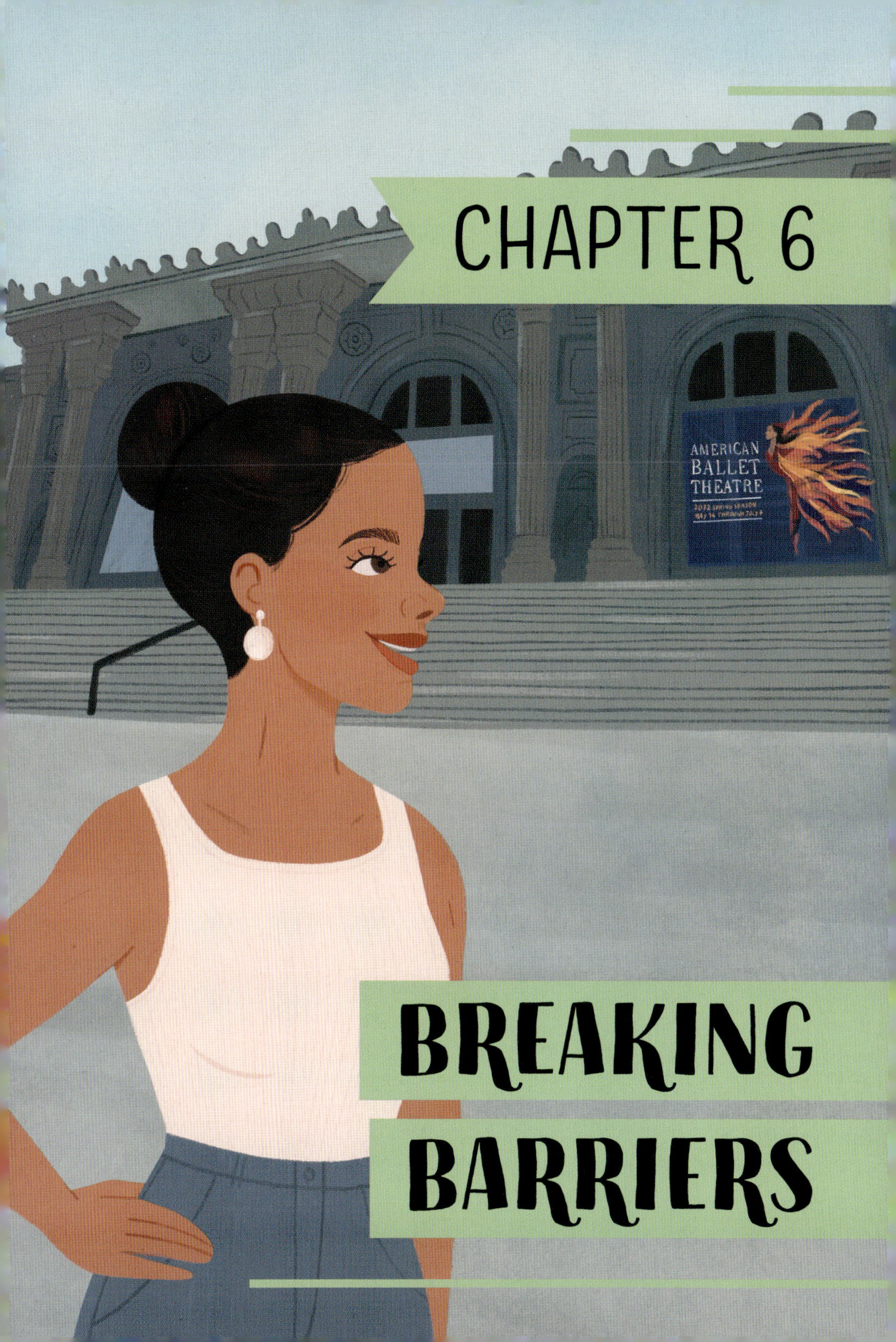

The Firebird

Misty had only been a soloist for four years when she started learning the part of the Firebird. *The Firebird* is a ballet about a prince who needs the help of a magical bird to save his true love. Misty assumed she would be an **understudy**. She was determined to be ready if she ever needed to fill in. But soon, Misty learned that she was not the understudy—she would perform the lead role! Misty would be the first Black woman in history to play the role of the Firebird for a major ballet company. It was a huge accomplishment. It also told the world that ballet was for everyone.

During rehearsals, Misty hurt her leg and told no one. She was afraid she would lose the role if someone found out. She also felt pressured to stay strong, because she was the only Black role model other ballerinas had to look up to. She tried to ignore the pain in her lower left leg as opening night drew closer. On the day of the show, Misty left the **dress rehearsal** in pain. But her spirits were lifted when she spotted herself on the 24-foot banner hanging outside the Metropolitan Opera House. It showed her in full costume as the Firebird. Misty had never seen a Black woman as the "face" of the Met before. Misty knew how proud it made people of color to see someone who looked like them up onstage.

Despite the growing pain in her leg, Misty knew she had to perform. On opening night, Misty took her place on the stage. When the curtain rose and the music began, her body, feet,

MYTH & FACT

MYTH	FACT
Ballerinas don't get hurt often.	Ballerinas get hurt all the time! They dance, jump, and push their bodies so much that injuries are not uncommon.

and mind took control. The years of training kicked in. Misty twisted, turned, and flew across the stage. The applause at the end was so loud, she could barely hear herself think!

Returning to the Stage

Two days after the performance, the pain in Misty's leg returned. After visiting the doctor, Misty learned she had six stress fractures in her lower leg! She was extremely upset. She had worked hard for many years to reach this point, and now her dancing career might be over. She began to wonder about life without ballet. What would she do if she could no longer dance?

After getting surgery on her leg, Misty found the strength to continue. Although she still couldn't walk, she started taking a floor **barre** class, which is a special type of ballet practice done without standing up. Misty would roll out of bed and do ballet while lying on the floor. Misty focused on her body and perfecting ballet moves. Although she was eager to return to the stage, she knew she still needed time to heal.

JUMP –IN THE– THINK TANK

Misty had big dreams and set goals to achieve them. Make a list of things you would like to do, then figure out how to reach those goals!

Misty stayed busy in other ways while she was recovering. She used her connections with the Boys & Girls Club and the ABT to create a program called Project Plié. Project Plié would bring trained ballet teachers to Boys & Girls Clubs across the country, in hopes of finding "the next Misty Copeland."

All the while, Misty never abandoned her dream of becoming a principal dancer, the highest rank at ABT. Just five months after surgery, Misty returned to classes and rehearsals. Two months later, she was back on stage! Misty didn't always receive praise for her dancing after her return. She began to understand that she couldn't please everyone. She simply had to give her best effort each and every time she took the stage.

In 2015, her dream came true! Misty made history when she became the first Black woman promoted to principal dancer at ABT!

WHEN?

2012	2014	2015
Misty dances the lead role in *The Firebird.*	Misty publishes two books, *Life in Motion* and *Firebird.*	Misty becomes a principal dancer at ABT.

CHAPTER 7

A DREAM COME TRUE

The Principal Role

By the time she was 18 (just five years after her first ballet lesson), Misty had joined ABT's Studio Company. Two years later, she was promoted to their corps de ballet. Six years later, she became a soloist. The company had not had a Black female soloist in over 20 years! Only the most talented performers reach the highest rank of principal dancer, so Misty was overjoyed when her dream finally came true at the age of 32.

Misty's fame continued to skyrocket after her history-making achievement. Her story was featured on news shows and in magazines around the world. As always, Misty stayed focused on becoming a better dancer. She wanted to show Black and brown girls that they could be strong, beautiful ballerinas, just like her.

As the first female African American principal dancer in the history of the ABT, Misty was a

JUMP —IN THE— THINK TANK

Misty overcame her fear to try new things, like ballet. Have you ever been afraid to try something new, like food, and then found out you loved it?

symbol of positive change. That spotlight gave her an opportunity to speak up about the lack of **diversity** in ballet. Misty wanted to introduce ballet to a wider audience. She continued to encourage new generations to learn more about the art form wherever she went.

In 2015, Misty performed *Swan Lake* with fellow dancer Brooklyn Mack. They made history as the first Black couple to play the lead roles in a full-length show. Misty also found time that year to dance in a Broadway play!

In 2016, Misty and Olu were married in California. They live in New York City so Misty can be within walking distance of the studios at ABT.

Misty also keeps busy offstage. She has written a biography, two children's books, and

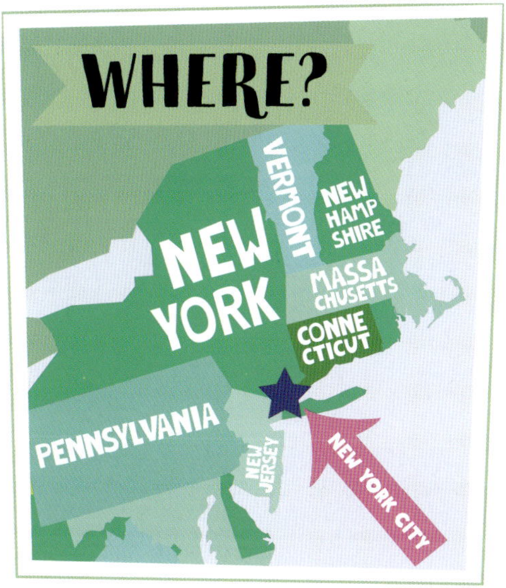

a health and fitness book. She also developed a successful line of athletic clothing called the Misty Copeland Signature Collection.

Misty loved Barbie® dolls as a child, so she was delighted when Mattel created a Misty Copeland doll based on the Firebird character!

★ Misty's Legacy ★

Misty Copeland has had an amazing life. As a child, she never could have imagined her incredible career as a world-class ballerina. Her love of dance has taken her to stages across the globe. Through years and years of hard work, she reached the highest levels of ballet.

Her history-making accomplishments continue to open doors for other Black and brown dancers.

Misty has never forgotten her humble beginnings. Ballet changed her life, and she believes it can do the same for others. She works with many organizations to bring ballet to children of color. She dedicates her free time to various charity events and donates money to scholarship funds.

Misty continues to be a role model to millions of little ballerinas (or bunheads, as they are lovingly called) who follow her every step, twist, and turn. Misty is an icon in the world of ballet, so there are crowds of fans wherever she goes!

> "I want to share this beautiful art form, which at its heart is so uplifting, with as many people possible because I know the joy and grace that it has given me."

She has broken many barriers, but her work is far from over! She created a program called Swans for Relief to raise funds for dancers whose shows were shut down due to the **pandemic** of 2020. She's also working on a book that celebrates Black ballerinas who came

before her and paved the way for her success. Misty is unstoppable—no one knows what this amazingly talented woman has planned next!

WHEN?

Misty hits Broadway in *On the Town.*

2015

Misty marries Olu.

2016

Misty publishes *Ballerina Body.*

2017

Misty creates Swans for Relief.

2020

CHAPTER 8

SO . . . WHO IS MISTY COPELAND?

Challenge Accepted!

Now that you know so much about Misty Copeland's amazing accomplishments, let's test your knowledge with a little who, what, when, where, why, and how quiz. Feel free to look back in the text to find the answers if you need to, but try to remember first.

1 Who is Misty Copeland?

- A A talented dancer and ballerina
- B A role model and trailblazer
- C An author and icon
- D All of the above

2 When was Misty born?

- A 1980
- B 1982
- C 1985
- D 1988

3 Where was Misty born?

- A Kansas City, Missouri
- B New York, New York
- C San Pedro, California
- D Los Angeles, California

4 How old was Misty when she started to study ballet?

- A 3
- B 7
- C 10
- D 13

5 Where did Misty take her first ballet class?

- A San Pedro Boys & Girls Club
- B San Pedro Ballet School
- C San Pedro Dance Center
- D Lauridsen Ballet Centre

6 **How many brothers and sisters does Misty have?**

- A 3
- B 4
- C 5
- D 0

7 **What company does Misty dance with?**

- A American Ballet Theatre
- B Dance Theatre of Harlem
- C San Francisco Ballet
- D New York City Ballet

8 **What is the name of Misty's childhood idol?**

- A Barack Obama
- B Kevin McKenzie
- C Arthur Mitchell
- D Paloma Herrera

9 **Misty performed on stage with which famous musician?**

→ A Mariah Carey

→ B Prince

→ C Backstreet Boys

→ D Justin Timberlake

10 **Misty has appeared in which of the following?**

→ A Movies

→ B Music videos

→ C A Broadway show

→ D All of the above

Answers: 1. D; 2. B; 3. A; 4. D; 5. A; 6. C; 7. A; 8. D; 9. B; 10. D

★ Our World ★

Misty has opened up the world of ballet to a much broader audience. Through her tireless work, she has introduced ballet to millions of new fans. Misty changed how ballerinas were seen! She proved that dancers could be any size, shape, or color. Misty is dedicated to changing the world through education, dance, and charity work.

→ Misty stands against **racism** and supports diversity both inside and outside of ballet. Some people ignored Misty's incredible talent because all they could see was her color.

→ Misty brings new faces to the stage *and* puts more diverse fans in the seats! As Misty's legacy continues to grow, more and more people of color have learned to appreciate ballet.

→ Misty gives back by donating her time and money. She promotes education through scholarships and dance, and works with various organizations to fight poverty around the world.

JUMP IN THE THINK TANK FOR MORE!

Misty wasn't afraid to have big dreams. She wanted to become a ballerina even though she had never seen one who looked like her. She wasn't afraid of new experiences. She was brave enough to pursue her dreams despite the many roadblocks and challenges she knew she would meet.

→ Misty was encouraged to take a ballet class, even though she knew very little about ballet. Is there something you may be good at but are afraid to try?

→ Misty was lucky to find people who wanted to help her succeed. Is there someone you can turn to when you need help? A good friend, parent, or teacher is a good start!

→ Misty was naturally talented, but she always believed in hard work. Do you work hard at school? If so, you're on track to success!

Glossary

ancestors: A person's parents, grandparents, and other relatives going back into history

appoint: To give someone a task or title

audition: To try out for a show as a performer

ballerina: A female dancer of ballet

ballet: A style of dance that uses specific positions

barre: A long horizontal pole used to practice ballet moves, keep balance, or stretch

choreograph: To create dance steps for a performance

classical: In a historically traditional style

culture: The way of life of a group of people, including their place of birth, food, language, clothing, music, art, beliefs, and religion

diversity: The state of including and giving equal representation to people of all races and cultures

divorce: The legal ending of a marriage between two people

dress rehearsal: A practice performance of a play or show onstage, in costume, exactly as it will be presented to an audience before it is seen

gymnastics: A sport in which athletes perform physical exercises on a mat or special equipment

lead: The main performer or star of a show

leotard: A one-piece bodysuit worn by dancers

pandemic: An outbreak of a disease that spreads very quickly and affects many people throughout the world

performance: The staging of a play or show

principal dancer: The highest-ranked dancer in a ballet company

racism: The discrimination of people of one race, by an individual or group that believes a different race is superior

scholarship: Money given to support a student's studies

siblings: Brothers and sisters

solo: A dance or music performance done alone, without a partner

solution: The answer to a problem

tights: The close-fitting, stretchy fabric covering dancers wear on their legs

understudy: A dancer who practices another dancer's role in case that dancer cannot perform

Bibliography

BOTWC staff. "BOTWC Firsts: Misty Copeland and Calvin Royal III will be the First Black Couple to Dance Lead Roles for the American Ballet Theatre." Because of Them We Can. January 16, 2019. BecauseOfThemWeCan.com/blogs/botwc-firsts/misty-copeland-and-calvin-royal-iii-will-be-the-first-black-couple-to-dance-lead-roles-for-the-american-ballet-theatre.

Copeland, Misty. *Bunheads*. New York: G.P. Putnam's Sons, 2020.

Copeland, Misty. *Life in Motion: An Unlikely Ballerina*. New York: Touchstone, 2014.

Copeland, Misty. Official Website. Accessed June 2021. MistyCopeland.com.

Glionna, John M. "Trapped in a Dispiriting Dance of Wills." *Los Angeles Times*. August 23, 1998. LATimes.com/archives/la-xpm-1998-aug-23-me-15815-story.html.

"Misty Copeland on Her Long Road to Ballet Stardom." *ABC News*. December 18, 2015. ABCNews.Go.com/Entertainment/video/misty-copeland-long-road-ballet-stardom-35833280.

Spencer Bell, Ian. "The Caramel Variations." *Ballet Review*. Dance Research Foundation, Inc. Spring 2012. BalletReview.com/images/Ballet_Review_40-1_Caramel_Variations.pdf.

About the Author

FRANK BERRIOS is a writer born in New York City. He is the author of *The Story of Joe Biden* and *The Story of Stan Lee*, as well as *A Little Golden Book about Jackie Robinson*, *Miles Morales: Spider-Man*, *Football with Dad*, and *Soccer with Mom*. Learn more about his work at FrankBerriosBooks.com.

About the Illustrator

JUANITA LONDOÑO is a children's book, editorial, and commercial illustrator from Medellín, Colombia. She has a degree in animation concept art from the Vancouver Film School. Juanita has worked for clients like Simon & Schuster, HarperCollins, Target, American Greetings, and Quarto. She likes drawing characters and environments with vibrant colors, textured details, and emotions to bring people on a journey. Juanita relishes seeing life through the lens of magical realism that is so deeply connected to her Latin American roots.

WHO WILL INSPIRE YOU NEXT?

EXPLORE A WORLD OF HEROES AND ROLE MODELS IN *THE STORY OF*... BIOGRAPHY SERIES FOR NEW READERS.

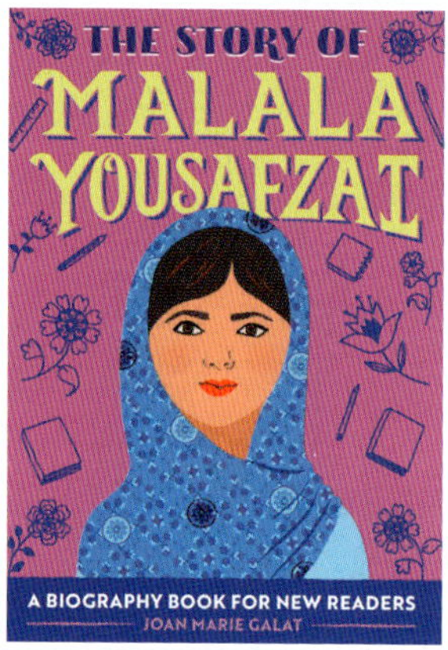

LOOK FOR THIS SERIES
WHEREVER BOOKS AND EBOOKS ARE SOLD

Alexander Hamilton
Albert Einstein
Martin Luther King Jr.
George Washington
Jane Goodall
Ruby Bridges
Helen Keller
Marie Curie